Space for Gratitude

SPACE FOR GRATITUDE

The Six-Minute Journal for Increased Happiness,
Gratitude, & Self-Understanding

Sonya Fehér

For Cavanaugh, Eben & Kobe
You are at the top of my gratitude list.

Table of Contents

In this body, in this town of spirit,
there is a little house shaped like a lotus,
and in that little house there is a space:

one should know what is there.
what is there? and why is it so important?

there is as much within that little space within the heart
as in the whole world…
whatever is, and whatever is not, everything is here.

– Chandogya Upanishad Ch. I

Introduction

I'm Happy You're Here

Welcome to *Space for Gratitude: The 6-Minute Journal for Increased Happiness, Gratitude, & Self-Understanding*. This book is designed to help you rewire your brain for happiness.

How could one book do that? It's not the journal that will make the change; it's your use of it. When you engage in a gratitude practice and take time to notice what makes you happy, you build new neural pathways—roads in your brain—that help you get to a different emotional destination.

Building a road in your brain initially wasn't a conscious process. For instance, when you had an experience like hearing a loud noise and you felt fear, the neurons for loud noise and fear fired together in your brain creating a link between that stimulus and response. As you continue to have the fear response each time you hear a loud noise, the link turns into a path, then a road, then the stimulus to response becomes so habitual that you've created ruts in your thinking.

Just as a tire can get stuck in a rut making it difficult to drive on a different part of the road, so can your thinking get stuck. It can feel like your thoughts, emotions, and reactions are out of your control, but they're likely a rut in your thinking. Your thoughts don't have to stay in this rut.

The great news is that you can build new positive roads by changing your response to a stimulus. You might notice that a loud noise is the car door outside signaling a loved one is home, or that the loud noise upstairs is a cat jumping off the bed and coming downstairs to wind around your ankles and purr. Each time you recognize that loud noise doesn't equal fear and, instead, is a positive event, you are firing off a different set of neurons, which changes your habitual response and helps the tire get out of the rut. When you pause to recognize that the loud bang is actually a cat coming to greet you or the car door of a loved one, you give your brain the information it needs to re-wire a new *happy* pathway and un-learn ruts.

Space for Gratitude offers you space to build new neural pathways as you engage in a daily practice of scanning for the positive. The journal consists of two main parts to help you do that: the daily pages and weekly happiness tools.

Daily Pages

The guided daily pages allow you to start the journal at any time of year. Unlike a dated journal, if you miss a day, you don't need to leave a gap that reminds you that you've missed a day. That's exactly the opposite of what you want to be doing. Instead, you pick up the journal and go right to the next page, adding the dates as you go.

The daily journaling will take six minutes or less: two minutes in the morning and four at night. As you answer the daily questions, you'll be practicing mindfulness – focusing your attention on the present moment. You'll scan for the positive, and in paying attention to what's good, you'll increase that goodness by hardwiring your brain for happiness.

The pages will give you space for:
- what you're looking forward to (anticipate the positive),
- what your goals and intentions for the day are (bring the emotions and actions you want into your day);
- when you feel happiest (reexperience the positive to fire the neurons again);
- whether anything distracts you or gets in the way of doing what you intended (notice potential for change);
- what you feel grateful for. There are many scientifically proven benefits of gratitude: improve physical and psychological health, build relationships, improve sleep,

2

enhance empathy, reduce aggression, and build mental strength among others;

- and what your plans are for the next day (combine intention and anticipation).

Weekly Happiness Tools

The weekly happiness tools will teach you gratitude, happiness, and mindfulness practices. These tools will take a little longer than the daily prompts: ten - twenty minutes depending upon the week. Each week will give you a new strategy for increasing the positive in your life from what you'd like mornings to look like, how much sleep your body needs, to the concept of enoughness, and the strategy of bookmarking happiness. The tools take practice, just as what you're doing with the daily pages does. As you're introduced to each one, you'll have new strategies that you can use. Some may be easier for you, while others will take longer to integrate. You can keep coming back to them. You may be surprised at how your answers change as you use the tools in your next *Space for Gratitude* journal.

More Tools

As a thank you for being here and to help you expand your gratitude practice, go to spacewiseorganizing.com/thankyougift to download 25 gratitude practices that you can use along with the journal or in your everyday life with family, friends, and random strangers out in the world. Enjoy!

Today, I'm looking forward to…

_____
_____
_____

Goals/Intentions for today:

_____
_____
_____

"Just where you are – that's the place to start."
– Pema Chödrön

I felt happiest today when…

_____
_____
_____

Diversions from what I intended …

_____
_____
_____

I'm grateful for…

_____
_____
_____

Plans for tomorrow:

_____   I am feeling:
_____
_____   ☺   ☺   ☹

4

Date: __/__/__

Today, I'm looking forward to…

_____
_____
_____

Goals/Intentions for today:

_____
_____
_____

"As you go along, you make up reasons to do what you want.
There's open space. Enter it."
− Natalie Goldberg

I felt happiest today when…

_____
_____
_____

Diversions from what I intended …

_____
_____
_____

I'm grateful for…

_____
_____
_____

Plans for tomorrow:

_____   I am feeling:
_____
_____   ☺   ☺   ☹

Date: __/__/__

Today, I'm looking forward to...

_____

_____

_____

Goals/Intentions for today:

_____

_____

_____

"Let yourself be drawn by the strange pull of what you really love.
It will not lead you astray."
– Rumi

I felt happiest today when...

_____

_____

_____

Diversions from what I intended ...

_____

_____

_____

I'm grateful for...

_____

_____

_____

Plans for tomorrow:

_____   I am feeling:

_____

_____   ☺   😐   ☹

6

Today, I'm looking forward to...

_____

_____

_____

Goals/Intentions for today:

_____

_____

_____

"The opposite of scarcity is not abundance.
The opposite of scarcity is simply enough. "
– Brené Brown

I felt happiest today when...

_____

_____

_____

Diversions from what I intended ...

_____

_____

_____

I'm grateful for...

_____

_____

_____

Plans for tomorrow:

_____   I am feeling:

_____

_____   ☺   😐   ☹

Date: __/__/__

Today, I'm looking forward to...

_____

_____

_____

Goals/Intentions for today:

_____

_____

_____

"Ever since happiness heard your name,
it has been running through the streets trying to find you."
– Hafiz

I felt happiest today when...

_____

_____

_____

Diversions from what I intended ...

_____

_____

_____

I'm grateful for...

_____

_____

_____

Plans for tomorrow:

_____   I am feeling:

_____

_____   ☺   😐   ☹

Date: __/__/__

Today, I'm looking forward to…

_____
_____
_____

Goals/Intentions for today:

_____
_____
_____

"The question is not what you look at, but what you see."
– Henry David Thoreau

I felt happiest today when…

_____
_____
_____

Diversions from what I intended …

_____
_____
_____

I'm grateful for…

_____
_____
_____

Plans for tomorrow:

_____   I am feeling:
_____
_____   ☺   ☺   ☹

Date: __/__/__

Today, I'm looking forward to…

_____

_____

_____

Goals/Intentions for today:

_____

_____

_____

"There are only seven days in the week and
'someday' is not one of them."
– Rita Chand

I felt happiest today when…

_____

_____

_____

Diversions from what I intended …

_____

_____

_____

I'm grateful for…

_____

_____

_____

Plans for tomorrow:

_____   I am feeling:

_____

_____   ☺   ☺   ☹

10

Define Happiness

Weekly Happiness Tool 1

Have you ever stopped to ask how you define happiness or even what being happy means for you? Take a few minutes right now. To help you come up with a working definition, answer any or all the following:

How do I know I'm happy?

_____

_____

_____

_____

_____

I am happy when…

_____

_____

_____

_____

Feeling happy includes…

_____

_____

_____

_____

_____

I am happy when I'm with…

_____

_____

_____

_____

I am happy doing…

_____

_____

_____

_____

I am happy being…

_____

_____

_____

_____

Writing a definition can be intimidating. Don't psyche yourself out here. Look back at your answers from above and write yourself a working definition of happiness. You'll have the chance to redefine happiness later in the book, so this is just your starting point.

My working definition of happiness is…

_____

_____

_____

_____

_____

_____

_____

_____

Today, I'm looking forward to…

_____

_____

_____

Goals/Intentions for today:

_____

_____

_____

"The here and now is all we have,
and if we play it right it's all we'll need."
– Ann Richards

I felt happiest today when…

_____

_____

_____

Diversions from what I intended …

_____

_____

_____

I'm grateful for…

_____

_____

_____

Plans for tomorrow:

_____   I am feeling:

_____

_____   ☺   ☺   ☹

Date: __/__/__

Today, I'm looking forward to…

_____

_____

_____

Goals/Intentions for today:

_____

_____

_____

"…the very least you can do in your life
is to figure out what you hope for.
And the most you can do is live inside that hope."
– Barbara Kingsolver

I felt happiest today when…

_____

_____

_____

Diversions from what I intended …

_____

_____

_____

I'm grateful for…

_____

_____

_____

Plans for tomorrow:

_____   I am feeling:

_____

_____   ☺   😐   ☹

14

Today, I'm looking forward to...

_____

_____

_____

Goals/Intentions for today:

_____

_____

_____

"When things get tough, how can you bring more grace to the table?"
– Adriene Mishler

I felt happiest today when...

_____

_____

_____

Diversions from what I intended ...

_____

_____

_____

I'm grateful for...

_____

_____

_____

Plans for tomorrow:

_____   I am feeling:

_____

_____   ☺   ☺   ☹

Date: __/__/__

Today, I'm looking forward to...

_____

_____

_____

Goals/Intentions for today:

_____

_____

_____

"The bottom of the world is gold and the world is upside down."
– Jack Kerouac

I felt happiest today when...

_____

_____

_____

Diversions from what I intended ...

_____

_____

_____

I'm grateful for...

_____

_____

_____

Plans for tomorrow:

_____   I am feeling:

_____

_____   ☺ ☺ ☹

16

Date: __/__/__

Today, I'm looking forward to...

_____

_____

_____

Goals/Intentions for today:

_____

_____

_____

"What one moment for you defines what it's like to be alive
on this planet? What's your takeaway?"
– Douglas Coupland

I felt happiest today when...

_____

_____

_____

Diversions from what I intended ...

_____

_____

_____

I'm grateful for...

_____

_____

_____

Plans for tomorrow:

_____   I am feeling:

_____

_____   ☺   ☺   ☹

17

Date: __/__/__

Today, I'm looking forward to...

_____

_____

_____

Goals/Intentions for today:

_____

_____

_____

"What's gonna set you free? Look inside and you'll see."
– Beastie Boys

I felt happiest today when...

_____

_____

_____

Diversions from what I intended ...

_____

_____

_____

I'm grateful for...

_____

_____

_____

Plans for tomorrow:

_____

_____   I am feeling:

_____   ☺   😐   ☹

Date: __/__/__

Today, I'm looking forward to...

_____

_____

_____

Goals/Intentions for today:

_____

_____

_____

"Each morning we are born again.
What we do today is what matters most."
– Buddha

I felt happiest today when...

_____

_____

_____

Diversions from what I intended ...

_____

_____

_____

I'm grateful for...

_____

_____

_____

Plans for tomorrow:

_____   I am feeling:

_____

_____   ☺   ☺   ☹

Bookmark Happiness

Weekly Happiness Tool 2

Another strategy for increasing happiness is to notice when you're happy and to "bookmark" that feeling. Bookmarks help you save your place in a book. Happiness bookmarks do the same thing. But instead of being able to find your page, bookmarking happiness means finding the feeling.

To bookmark happiness, stop and notice when you're feeling happy. Take it in. You might say to yourself, *"I feel happy right now because...."* Mentally bookmarking happiness is about taking an extra moment when you're enjoying something to notice that you're enjoying it.

Ultimately, bookmarking happiness is a mindfulness practice. Rather than being stuck in thoughts of the past or the future, when you bookmark happiness, you bring yourself into the present moment. You get to be right here, right now—feeling happy.

As you fill out your "I felt happiest today" section of the daily pages, you're revisiting happy feelings you mentally bookmarked throughout that day.

Date: __/__/__

Today, I'm looking forward to…

_____

_____

_____

Goals/Intentions for today:

_____

_____

_____

"Keep what is worth keeping —
and with the breath of kindness blow the rest away."
– Dinah Mulock Craik

I felt happiest today when…

_____

_____

_____

Diversions from what I intended …

_____

_____

_____

I'm grateful for…

_____

_____

_____

Plans for tomorrow:

_____

_____   I am feeling:

_____   ☺   😐   ☹

Date: __/__/__

Today, I'm looking forward to…

_____

_____

_____

Goals/Intentions for today:

_____

_____

_____

"What a wonderful thought it is that
some of the best days of our lives haven't even happened yet."
– Anne Frank

I felt happiest today when…

_____

_____

_____

Diversions from what I intended …

_____

_____

_____

I'm grateful for…

_____

_____

_____

Plans for tomorrow:

_____   I am feeling:

_____

_____   ☺   ☺   ☹

Date: __/__/__

Today, I'm looking forward to...

_____

_____

_____

Goals/Intentions for today:

_____

_____

_____

*"That the birds of worry and care fly above your head, this you cannot change.
But that they build their nests in your hair, this you can prevent."*
– Chinese Proverb

I felt happiest today when...

_____

_____

_____

Diversions from what I intended ...

_____

_____

_____

I'm grateful for...

_____

_____

_____

Plans for tomorrow:

_____   I am feeling:

_____

_____   ☺   ☺   ☹

Date: __/__/__

Today, I'm looking forward to…

_____

_____

_____

Goals/Intentions for today:

_____

_____

_____

"Real luxury is not working like a maniac to take an expensive vacation —
it is living a life you enjoy every day."
– Kathy Gottberg

I felt happiest today when…

_____

_____

_____

Diversions from what I intended …

_____

_____

_____

I'm grateful for…

_____

_____

_____

Plans for tomorrow:

_____   I am feeling:

_____

_____   ☺   ☺   ☹

24

Date: __/__/__

Today, I'm looking forward to...

_____

_____

_____

Goals/Intentions for today:

_____

_____

_____

"Comparison is the thief of joy."
— Theodore Roosevelt

I felt happiest today when...

_____

_____

_____

Diversions from what I intended ...

_____

_____

_____

I'm grateful for...

_____

_____

_____

Plans for tomorrow:

_____   I am feeling:

_____

_____   ☺   😐   ☹

Date: __/__/__

Today, I'm looking forward to…

_____

_____

_____

Goals/Intentions for today:

_____

_____

_____

"All of us could take a lesson from the weather.
It pays no attention to criticism."
– North Dekalb

I felt happiest today when…

_____

_____

_____

Diversions from what I intended …

_____

_____

_____

I'm grateful for…

_____

_____

_____

Plans for tomorrow:

_____   I am feeling:

_____

_____   ☺   ☺   ☹

Date: __/__/__

Today, I'm looking forward to...

_____

_____

_____

Goals/Intentions for today:

_____

_____

_____

"How we spend our days is, of course, how we spend our lives."
– Annie Dillard

I felt happiest today when...

_____

_____

_____

Diversions from what I intended ...

_____

_____

_____

I'm grateful for...

_____

_____

_____

Plans for tomorrow:

_____

_____   I am feeling:

_____   ☺ 😐 ☹

27

Recognize When You're Out of Balance

Weekly Happiness Tool 3

While being centered—feeling like your life is in balance—doesn't guarantee happiness, it sure helps. It's harder to be happy when your life is out of balance because you may feel stressed, rushed, or just out of sorts. However, it's hard to fix something if we don't know anything's wrong and being out of balance often includes not even noticing when the scales have tipped.

This week consider what it looks and feels like when your life is out of balance. Simply recognizing when there's a problem goes a long way towards solving it. Next week, I'll teach you strategies for getting back to center when you recognize that things are out of balance.

Being off-center can take many forms: an overly busy schedule, so much focus on other people that you're not taking care of yourself, or circumstances that take you out of your regular routine like illness, the holidays, or a trip. Maybe it's not so much that things are out of balance now as that they weren't ever in balance because you struggle with organization, routines, or just don't know what being in balance would look like for you.

Whether being out of balance is a temporary state or where you live every day, recognizing what it looks and feels like to be out of balance is your happiness tool this week, a strategy you can employ anytime.

So, what are the signs that you're not in balance at the moment? Some of them may be external—the state of your car, home, or calendar; not seeing friends; or engaging in comfort activities like binge-watching TV, losing time on social media, or eating comfort food. Other signs might be skipping daily habits like exercise or meditation. Some signs may be more internal like having a hard time falling asleep, clenching your teeth, constant low-level stress with all that you have on your to do list.

What are the external signs in your home or other spaces that you or your life are out of balance?

_____

_____

_____

What indicators are there in your interactions with others?

_____

_____

_____

Are there self-care or other important habits that you neglect? If so, what are they?

_____

_____

_____

Write down anything else that signals things aren't so okay.

_____

_____

_____

_____

_____

_____

_____

Date: __/__/__

Today, I'm looking forward to...

_____

_____

_____

Goals/Intentions for today:

_____

_____

_____

"The beginning is always today."
– Mary Wollstonecraft Shelley

I felt happiest today when...

_____

_____

_____

Diversions from what I intended ...

_____

_____

_____

I'm grateful for...

_____

_____

_____

Plans for tomorrow:

_____   I am feeling:

_____

_____   ☺   😐   ☹

Today, I'm looking forward to...

_____

_____

_____

Goals/Intentions for today:

_____

_____

_____

"Joy is not in things; it is in us."
– Richard Wagner

I felt happiest today when...

_____

_____

_____

Diversions from what I intended ...

_____

_____

_____

I'm grateful for...

_____

_____

_____

Plans for tomorrow:

_____   I am feeling:

_____

_____   ☺   ☺   ☹

31

Date: __/__/__

Today, I'm looking forward to…

_____

_____

_____

Goals/Intentions for today:

_____

_____

_____

"Money does not buy you freedom. Time does."
– J.R. Rim

I felt happiest today when…

_____

_____

_____

Diversions from what I intended …

_____

_____

_____

I'm grateful for…

_____

_____

_____

Plans for tomorrow:

_____   I am feeling:

_____

_____   ☺ 😐 ☹

Date: __/__/__

Today, I'm looking forward to…

_____
_____
_____

Goals/Intentions for today:

_____
_____
_____

"Change your thoughts and you can change your world."
– Norman Vincent Peale

I felt happiest today when…

_____
_____
_____

Diversions from what I intended …

_____
_____
_____

I'm grateful for…

_____
_____
_____

Plans for tomorrow:

_____   I am feeling:
_____
_____   ☺   ☻   ☹

33

Date: __/__/__

Today, I'm looking forward to...

_____

_____

_____

Goals/Intentions for today:

_____

_____

_____

"It's a funny thing about life, once you begin to take note of the things you are grateful for, you begin to lose sight of the things that you lack."
– Germany Kent

I felt happiest today when...

_____

_____

_____

Diversions from what I intended ...

_____

_____

_____

I'm grateful for...

_____

_____

_____

Plans for tomorrow:

_____   I am feeling:

_____

_____   ☺ ☺ ☹

Date: __/__/__

Today, I'm looking forward to...

_____

_____

_____

Goals/Intentions for today:

_____

_____

_____

"It is not enough to have a good mind.
The main thing is to use it well."
– René Descartes

I felt happiest today when...

_____

_____

_____

Diversions from what I intended ...

_____

_____

_____

I'm grateful for...

_____

_____

_____

Plans for tomorrow:

_____   I am feeling:

_____

_____   ☺   😐   ☹

35

Date: __/__/__

Today, I'm looking forward to...

_____

_____

_____

Goals/Intentions for today:

_____

_____

_____

"It doesn't matter how well you walk the path if it's not your path."
– Katherine Benzinger

I felt happiest today when...

_____

_____

_____

Diversions from what I intended ...

_____

_____

_____

I'm grateful for...

_____

_____

_____

Plans for tomorrow:

_____   I am feeling:

_____

_____   ☺   ☻   ☹

Centering

Weekly Happiness Tool 4

What helps you get back to center when your life is out of balance? Is it about what you eat, how much you sleep, who you see, or something else?

You might look both at what you are doing and what you're not doing, then make a switch. If you're not getting enough sleep, water, healthy food, social time, time alone, work time, or something else, how can you create some space for that?

Alternately, you might get back to center by stopping whatever's throwing you off balance. For instance, you could turn off electronics if the screen time is taking away from other things. If your schedule is too full, you might look at your calendar to see if you can cancel or reschedule something to a later date. Or, you can go through your to-do list and evaluate whether any of the tasks can be delegated, deleted, or moved to another day, week, or month. If being around a particular person throws you off, you can take a little break, schedule a different kind of time with them, or talk to them and see if you can change your relationship dynamic.

Another strategy is to have go-to centering methods so that you when you need centering the most, you've got a resource rather than having to think about or create something in the moment. You can use these centering exercises when you're feeling off-balance, anxious, angry, you're spinning, or when you're doing any of the things you noted in the Week Three exercise for noticing when you're off balance.

Here are some centering strategies to help in the moment:

- Go outside and look up
- Drink water
- Take three slow deep breaths. If you need more, take more.
- Smell something calming (lavender essential oil is a good one)
- Walk around the block
- Turn off electronics
- Turn on music
- Go to bed
- Spend some time alone
- Clean up
- Reach out to someone
- Meditate

Your turn. What are some things you know work well to help you get re-centered when you're out of balance?

_____

_____

_____

_____

_____

_____

_____

_____

_____

_____

_____

Date: __/__/__

Today, I'm looking forward to...

_____

_____

_____

Goals/Intentions for today:

_____

_____

_____

"Almost everything will work again
if you unplug it for a few minutes, including you."
– Anne Lamott

I felt happiest today when...

_____

_____

_____

Diversions from what I intended ...

_____

_____

_____

I'm grateful for...

_____

_____

_____

Plans for tomorrow:

_____   I am feeling:

_____

_____   ☺   ☺   ☹

Date: __/__/__

Today, I'm looking forward to…

_____

_____

_____

Goals/Intentions for today:

_____

_____

_____

"When you are willing to listen and to learn,
even the stones speak."
– Lazarus

I felt happiest today when…

_____

_____

_____

Diversions from what I intended …

_____

_____

_____

I'm grateful for…

_____

_____

_____

Plans for tomorrow:

_____   I am feeling:

_____

_____   ☺   ☺   ☹

Today, I'm looking forward to…

_____

_____

_____

Goals/Intentions for today:

_____

_____

_____

"If you feel like dancing, Dance, for we are free."
– Bob Marley

I felt happiest today when…

_____

_____

_____

Diversions from what I intended …

_____

_____

_____

I'm grateful for…

_____

_____

_____

Plans for tomorrow:

_____   I am feeling:

_____

_____   ☺   ☺   ☹

Date: __/__/__

Today, I'm looking forward to...

_____

_____

_____

Goals/Intentions for today:

_____

_____

_____

"There's a capacity for appetite...
that a whole heaven and earth of cake can't satisfy."
– John Steinbeck

I felt happiest today when...

_____

_____

_____

Diversions from what I intended ...

_____

_____

_____

I'm grateful for...

_____

_____

_____

Plans for tomorrow:

_____   I am feeling:

_____

_____   ☺   ☺   ☹

Date: __/__/__

Today, I'm looking forward to…

_____

_____

_____

Goals/Intentions for today:

_____

_____

_____

"Cry. Forgive. Learn. Move on.
Let your tears water the seeds of your future happiness."
– Steve Maraboli

I felt happiest today when…

_____

_____

_____

Diversions from what I intended …

_____

_____

_____

I'm grateful for…

_____

_____

_____

Plans for tomorrow:

_____   I am feeling:

_____

_____   ☺   😐   ☹

Date: __/__/__

Today, I'm looking forward to…

_____

_____

_____

Goals/Intentions for today:

_____

_____

_____

"In the depth of winter, I finally learned
that within me lay an invincible summer."
– Albert Camus

I felt happiest today when…

_____

_____

_____

Diversions from what I intended …

_____

_____

_____

I'm grateful for…

_____

_____

_____

Plans for tomorrow:

_____   I am feeling:

_____

_____   ☺   😐   ☹

Today, I'm looking forward to...

_____

_____

_____

Goals/Intentions for today:

_____

_____

_____

"It is never too late to be what you might have been."
– George Eliot

I felt happiest today when...

_____

_____

_____

Diversions from what I intended ...

_____

_____

_____

I'm grateful for...

_____

_____

_____

Plans for tomorrow:

_____   I am feeling:

_____

_____   ☺   😐   ☹

Make a Play List

Weekly Happiness Tool 5

For the last four weeks, you've been noticing what you're grateful for and what makes you happy, setting daily intentions, and considering what might distract you from what you intended. In other words, you've been doing some big work. This week let's play.

Your happiness tool this week is to make a play list, not the musical kind, though putting on something to listen to while you do this could be great. What I want you to do this week is think about all of the ways you like to play and make a list of things that you like to do for fun, things that make you happy, that are play in its truest sense—activity for enjoyment and recreation rather than a serious or practical purpose.

Making a play list is a way of getting to know yourself and of giving yourself a go-to resource for ways to spend your time. It's easy to get into routines and to forget to add in the extra fun. Having a list posted on a wall, on your phone, or by your calendar can serve as a reminder to schedule in some play. You can also refer to your play list when you're in a funk and need a way to get out of it but aren't in the mood to think of anything you enjoy now or ever have.

You're creating your own happiness tool this week. Make a list of 50 fun things. You can write them all in one sitting. You could keep a running list that you add to over time. You can look at what kinds of outings and activities you've put on your calendar in the last few months. Or, think about what you wish you'd had on your calendar. You can ask friends what they like to do for fun and check in with yourself to see if you'd want those things on your list too.

To help you brainstorm, consider the following: What can you do for fun in 5, 15, or 30 minutes, three hours, one day, or one weekend? What can you do inside, outside, with others, by yourself, that costs money, that is free, in this season, in this town, etc.?

1. _____
2. _____
3. _____
4. _____
5. _____
6. _____
7. _____
8. _____
9. _____
10. _____
11. _____
12. _____
13. _____
14. _____
15. _____
16. _____
17. _____
18. _____
19. _____
20. _____
21. _____
22. _____
23. _____
24. _____
25. _____
26. _____
27. _____

28. _____
29. _____
30. _____
31. _____
32. _____
33. _____
34. _____
35. _____
36. _____
37. _____
38. _____
39. _____
40. _____
41. _____
42. _____
43. _____
44. _____
45. _____
46. _____
47. _____
48. _____
49. _____
50. _____

Date: __/__/__

Today, I'm looking forward to…

_____

_____

_____

Goals/Intentions for today:

_____

_____

_____

"When I started counting my blessings,
my whole life turned around."
– Willie Nelson

I felt happiest today when…

_____

_____

_____

Diversions from what I intended …

_____

_____

_____

I'm grateful for…

_____

_____

_____

Plans for tomorrow:

_____   I am feeling:

_____

_____   ☺   😐   ☹

Today, I'm looking forward to…

_____

_____

_____

Goals/Intentions for today:

_____

_____

_____

"I said 'Somebody should do something about that.'
Then I realized, I am somebody."
– Lily Tomlin

I felt happiest today when…

_____

_____

_____

Diversions from what I intended …

_____

_____

_____

I'm grateful for…

_____

_____

_____

Plans for tomorrow:

_____   I am feeling:

_____

_____   ☺   ☺   ☹

Date: __/__/__

Today, I'm looking forward to…

_____

_____

_____

Goals/Intentions for today:

_____

_____

_____

"It's time to start living the life you've imagined."
– Henry James

I felt happiest today when…

_____

_____

_____

Diversions from what I intended …

_____

_____

_____

I'm grateful for…

_____

_____

_____

Plans for tomorrow:

_____   I am feeling:

_____

_____   ☺   ☺   ☹

51

Date: __/__/__

Today, I'm looking forward to...

_____

_____

_____

Goals/Intentions for today:

_____

_____

_____

"Pursuit of contentment is not the pursuit of an elusive tomorrow;
it is the celebration of today."
– Majid Kazmi

I felt happiest today when...

_____

_____

_____

Diversions from what I intended ...

_____

_____

_____

I'm grateful for...

_____

_____

_____

Plans for tomorrow:

_____   I am feeling:

_____

_____   ☺   ☺   ☹

Date: __/__/__

Today, I'm looking forward to…

_____

_____

_____

Goals/Intentions for today:

_____

_____

_____

"Forever is composed of Nows."
– Emily Dickinson

I felt happiest today when…

_____

_____

_____

Diversions from what I intended …

_____

_____

_____

I'm grateful for…

_____

_____

_____

Plans for tomorrow:

_____   I am feeling:

_____

_____   ☺   ☺   ☹

Date: __/__/__

Today, I'm looking forward to…

_____

_____

_____

Goals/Intentions for today:

_____

_____

_____

"You can have it all. Just not all at once."
– Oprah Winfrey

I felt happiest today when…

_____

_____

_____

Diversions from what I intended …

_____

_____

_____

I'm grateful for…

_____

_____

_____

Plans for tomorrow:

_____   I am feeling:

_____

_____   ☺   ☺   ☹

Date: __/__/__

Today, I'm looking forward to…

_____

_____

_____

Goals/Intentions for today:

_____

_____

_____

"Now and then it's good to pause in our pursuit of happiness
and just be happy."
– Guillaume Apollinaire

I felt happiest today when…

_____

_____

_____

Diversions from what I intended …

_____

_____

_____

I'm grateful for…

_____

_____

_____

Plans for tomorrow:

_____   I am feeling:

_____

_____   ☺ ☺ ☹

55

Recognize Diversions

Weekly Happiness Tool 6

On your daily journal pages, what repeats in your "diversions from what I intended" section? These could be distractions, emergencies, unplanned for activities, or something else. What is it that gets in the way of you doing what you intended to on any given day?

_____   _____

_____   _____

_____   _____

_____   _____

Are they things you wish you had done or that you hadn't?

_____

_____

_____

_____

_____

What would you need to change or do so that these diversions don't continue to divert you? This is an opportunity for habit change.

_____

_____

_____

_____

Date: __/__/__

Today, I'm looking forward to…

_____

_____

_____

Goals/Intentions for today:

_____

_____

_____

*"Happiness is exercising the little freedom that we have
by choosing things that create harmony in our lives."*
– Kamand Kojouri

I felt happiest today when…

_____

_____

_____

Diversions from what I intended …

_____

_____

_____

I'm grateful for…

_____

_____

_____

Plans for tomorrow:

_____   I am feeling:

_____

_____   ☺   ☺   ☹

57

Date: __/__/__

Today, I'm looking forward to...

_____
_____
_____

Goals/Intentions for today:

_____
_____
_____

"Tell me, what is it you plan to do
with your one wild and precious life?"
– Mary Oliver

I felt happiest today when...

_____
_____
_____

Diversions from what I intended ...

_____
_____
_____

I'm grateful for...

_____
_____
_____

Plans for tomorrow:

_____   I am feeling:
_____
_____   ☺   ☺   ☹

Today, I'm looking forward to...

_____

_____

_____

Goals/Intentions for today:

_____

_____

_____

"Nothing is worth more than this day."
– Johann Wolfgang von Goethe

I felt happiest today when...

_____

_____

_____

Diversions from what I intended ...

_____

_____

_____

I'm grateful for...

_____

_____

_____

Plans for tomorrow:

_____   I am feeling:

_____

_____   ☺   ☺   ☹

Date: __/__/__

Today, I'm looking forward to…

_____

_____

_____

Goals/Intentions for today:

_____

_____

_____

"This very moment is the perfect teacher,
and, lucky for us, it's with us wherever we go."
– Pema Chödrön

I felt happiest today when…

_____

_____

_____

Diversions from what I intended …

_____

_____

_____

I'm grateful for…

_____

_____

_____

Plans for tomorrow:

_____   I am feeling:

_____

_____   ☺   ☺   ☹

Date: __/__/__

Today, I'm looking forward to…

_____
_____
_____

Goals/Intentions for today:

_____
_____
_____

"In the middle of the journey of our life I came to myself in a dark wood where the straight way was lost."
– Dante Alighieri

I felt happiest today when…

_____
_____
_____

Diversions from what I intended …

_____
_____
_____

I'm grateful for…

_____
_____
_____

Plans for tomorrow:

_____   I am feeling:
_____
_____   ☺   ☺   ☹

Date: __/__/__

Today, I'm looking forward to…

_____

_____

_____

Goals/Intentions for today:

_____

_____

_____

*"There are two ways to get enough.
One is to continue to accumulate more and more.
The other is to desire less."*
– G.K. Chesterton

I felt happiest today when…

_____

_____

_____

Diversions from what I intended …

_____

_____

_____

I'm grateful for…

_____

_____

_____

Plans for tomorrow:

_____   I am feeling:

_____

_____   ☺   ☺   ☹

Date: __/__/__

Today, I'm looking forward to…

_____

_____

_____

Goals/Intentions for today:

_____

_____

_____

"And suddenly you know: It's time to start something new
and trust the magic of beginnings."
– Meister Eckhart

I felt happiest today when…

_____

_____

_____

Diversions from what I intended …

_____

_____

_____

I'm grateful for…

_____

_____

_____

Plans for tomorrow:

_____   I am feeling:

_____

_____   ☺   ☺   ☹

63

Envision Your Good Morning

Weekly Happiness Tool 7

How you start your day sets the tone for the rest of it. Hitting snooze, skipping breakfast, searching for your keys, being sidetracked by email or other notifications, and many more things can derail your day before it's really begun.

What would a *good* morning include? If you had complete control of the circumstances—no alarm to wake up to, no one else to take care of, no time you had to be someplace—how would you structure your mornings?

You may be thinking that's not reality land at all. What can happen if you visualize your perfect morning is that you can then figure out how to structure your actual life to allow for some or all of what a good morning for you would mean.

So, go with me for a minute in visualizing this good morning. Think of this not as a vacation day or a weekend. Instead, consider how you would start your day if you worked for yourself and could be completely in charge of your schedule.

How many hours do you want to sleep a night (most experts recommend seven to nine hours a night for adults)? _____

How would you feel upon waking, when you're still lying in bed?

_____

_____

Would you do anything before you get out of bed (stretch, read, bookmark happiness, etc.)?

_____

_____

Would you exercise in the morning, and if so, what would you do and for how long? Include travel time, if necessary.

_____

_____

How much time would you like for shower or bath, getting dressed and getting your body ready (hair, shaving, etc.)?

_____

_____

_____

Would you engage in any contemplative activities (meditation, prayer, reading, writing)? If so, which ones and for how long?

_____

_____

_____

How about food and drink? What would a good nutritional start to the day include and how long would you allow for food prep and eating?

_____

_____

_____

Is there anything else you'd want to do as part of your daily morning routine before the rest of your day begins?

_____

_____

_____

How could you structure the start of your day so that it includes as much of what you listed above as possible? Would it mean setting the alarm earlier? Could it mean doing some of the things you normally do in the morning the night before so that you can have more time for how you really want to start your day?

_____

_____

_____

_____

_____

_____

_____

_____

_____

Look back at the previous page and what you've written just above and pick one thing to change, even if it's setting the alarm just ten minutes earlier. What are you going to try?

_____

_____

_____

_____

Date: __/__/__

Today, I'm looking forward to…

_____

_____

_____

Goals/Intentions for today:

_____

_____

_____

"I am not a product of my circumstances.
I am a product of my decisions."
– Stephen Covey

I felt happiest today when…

_____

_____

_____

Diversions from what I intended …

_____

_____

_____

I'm grateful for…

_____

_____

_____

Plans for tomorrow:

_____   I am feeling:

_____

_____   ☺ ☺ ☹

Date: __/__/__

Today, I'm looking forward to...

_____

_____

_____

Goals/Intentions for today:

_____

_____

_____

"It's never too late - in fiction or in life - to revise."
– Nancy Thayer

I felt happiest today when...

_____

_____

_____

Diversions from what I intended ...

_____

_____

_____

I'm grateful for...

_____

_____

_____

Plans for tomorrow:

_____   I am feeling:

_____

_____   ☺   😐   ☹

68

Date: __/__/__

Today, I'm looking forward to...

_____

_____

_____

Goals/Intentions for today:

_____

_____

_____

"Life isn't about finding yourself. Life is about creating yourself."
– George Bernard Shaw

I felt happiest today when...

_____

_____

_____

Diversions from what I intended ...

_____

_____

_____

I'm grateful for...

_____

_____

_____

Plans for tomorrow:

_____

_____

_____

I am feeling:

☺   😐   ☹

Date: __/__/__

Today, I'm looking forward to...

_____

_____

_____

Goals/Intentions for today:

_____

_____

_____

"Keep in mind always the present you are constructing.
It should be the future you want."
– Alice Walker

I felt happiest today when...

_____

_____

_____

Diversions from what I intended ...

_____

_____

_____

I'm grateful for...

_____

_____

_____

Plans for tomorrow:

_____   I am feeling:

_____

_____   ☺   😐   ☹

Date: __/__/__

Today, I'm looking forward to…

_____

_____

_____

Goals/Intentions for today:

_____

_____

_____

"These mountains that you are carrying,
you were only supposed to climb."
– Najwa Zebian

I felt happiest today when…

_____

_____

_____

Diversions from what I intended …

_____

_____

_____

I'm grateful for…

_____

_____

_____

Plans for tomorrow:

_____   I am feeling:

_____

_____   ☺   ☺   ☹

71

Date: __/__/__

Today, I'm looking forward to...

_____

_____

_____

Goals/Intentions for today:

_____

_____

_____

"Nothing can bring you peace but yourself."
– R.W. Emerson

I felt happiest today when...

_____

_____

_____

Diversions from what I intended ...

_____

_____

_____

I'm grateful for...

_____

_____

_____

Plans for tomorrow:

_____   I am feeling:

_____

_____   ☺   😐   ☹

Date: __/__/__

Today, I'm looking forward to…

_____

_____

_____

Goals/Intentions for today:

_____

_____

_____

"Silence, I discover, is something you can actually hear."
– Harukami Murakami

I felt happiest today when…

_____

_____

_____

Diversions from what I intended …

_____

_____

_____

I'm grateful for…

_____

_____

_____

Plans for tomorrow:

_____   I am feeling:

_____

_____   ☺   😐   ☹

Get Enough Rest: Good Nights

Weekly Happiness Tool 8

Getting enough sleep is associated with better physical and mental health, more mental clarity, ability to process memory and experiences, and so much more.

Our bodies are designed so that fully one-third of our lives will be spent sleeping. Rather than considering it a waste of time or foregoing sleep for a myriad of reasons, one happiness tool is to structure your time so that you get the amount of sleep your body needs to operate optimally. If you're chronically sleep-deprived, take a few minutes to figure out how you can change that. And if you're getting enough rest (good, deep, restorative sleep with dreams), woo hoo! Good for you. You can skip this exercise and get back to journaling.

How many hours of sleep does your body need (most experts recommend seven to nine hours a night for adults)? _____

What's getting in the way of your getting enough sleep or good sleep?
- ☐ Staying on screens: TV, computer, social media, etc.
- ☐ Being too tired to put yourself to bed
- ☐ Not winding down before bed
- ☐ Work
- ☐ Other people in the household
- ☐ Noise
- ☐ Insomnia
- ☐ Too much caffeine earlier in day

- ☐ Shift work
- ☐ Eating and drinking late
- ☐ Alcohol, drugs, sleeping pills, or other inhibitors of REM sleep
- ☐ Stress
- ☐ Medical conditions including pregnancy
- ☐ Waiting for others to go to bed so you can get alone time
- ☐ Other:_____
- ☐ Other:_____
- ☐ Other:_____

Now that you've identified the reason(s) you're not getting enough rest, take the steps to help yourself sleep. Set an alarm to get off screens, stop working, clean up the house, put others to bed or otherwise give yourself a window to be able to wind down before bed. Consider your use of caffeine, intoxicants, and other deep sleep inhibitors (including, ironically, sleeping pills). If you need sleeping pills, think about what's causing you to need them—caffeine, insomnia, stress, sleep apnea, pain, etc.—and see a health practitioner or otherwise take steps to get the help you'd need to sleep without sleep aids.

Just as you imagined a good morning, picture a good end to your day. What would it include and how could you structure your time so you would get to bed on time and be able to sleep?

_____

_____

_____

_____

_____

_____

_____

_____

Date: __/__/__

Today, I'm looking forward to...

_____

_____

_____

Goals/Intentions for today:

_____

_____

_____

"Time is a created thing. To say, 'I don't have time'
is to say, 'I don't want to'."
– Lao Tzu

I felt happiest today when...

_____

_____

_____

Diversions from what I intended ...

_____

_____

_____

I'm grateful for...

_____

_____

_____

Plans for tomorrow:

_____   I am feeling:

_____

_____   ☺   ☺   ☹

Date: __/__/__

Today, I'm looking forward to…

_____

_____

_____

Goals/Intentions for today:

_____

_____

_____

"I shall tell you a great secret, my friend. Do not wait for the last judgment.
It takes place every day."
– Albert Camus

I felt happiest today when…

_____

_____

_____

Diversions from what I intended …

_____

_____

_____

I'm grateful for…

_____

_____

_____

Plans for tomorrow:

_____   I am feeling:

_____

_____   ☺   😐   ☹

Date: __/__/__

Today, I'm looking forward to...

_____

_____

_____

Goals/Intentions for today:

_____

_____

_____

"Stop a minute, right where you are. Relax your shoulders,
shake your head and spine like a dog shaking off cold water.
Tell that imperious voice in your head to be still."
– Barbara Kingsolver

I felt happiest today when...

_____

_____

_____

Diversions from what I intended ...

_____

_____

_____

I'm grateful for...

_____

_____

_____

Plans for tomorrow:

_____   I am feeling:

_____

_____   ☺ ☺ ☹

Date: __/__/__

Today, I'm looking forward to…

_____

_____

_____

Goals/Intentions for today:

_____

_____

_____

"…the world is turning faster
than it did when I was young."
– Rickie Lee Jones

I felt happiest today when…

_____

_____

_____

Diversions from what I intended …

_____

_____

_____

I'm grateful for…

_____

_____

_____

Plans for tomorrow:

_____

I am feeling:

_____

_____

☺   ☺   ☹

79

Date: __/__/__

Today, I'm looking forward to…

_____

_____

_____

Goals/Intentions for today:

_____

_____

_____

"Look at everything always as though you were seeing it either for the first or last time."
– Betty Smith

I felt happiest today when…

_____

_____

_____

Diversions from what I intended …

_____

_____

_____

I'm grateful for…

_____

_____

_____

Plans for tomorrow:

_____   I am feeling:

_____

_____   ☺   ☺   ☹

80

Date: __/__/__

Today, I'm looking forward to…

_____

_____

_____

Goals/Intentions for today:

_____

_____

_____

"You've got only one life to live, and you don't have to live it for six people.
Pay attention to it."
– Joseph Campbell

I felt happiest today when…

_____

_____

_____

Diversions from what I intended …

_____

_____

_____

I'm grateful for…

_____

_____

_____

Plans for tomorrow:

_____   I am feeling:

_____

_____   ☺   ☺   ☹

Today, I'm looking forward to…

_____

_____

_____

Goals/Intentions for today:

_____

_____

_____

"…to belong to oneself, that is the whole thing in life."
– Ivan Turgenev

I felt happiest today when…

_____

_____

_____

Diversions from what I intended …

_____

_____

_____

I'm grateful for…

_____

_____

_____

Plans for tomorrow:

_____   I am feeling:

_____

_____   ☺ ☻ ☹

Consider What If Vs. What Is

Weekly Happiness Tool 9

One secret to happiness is accepting *what is* instead of living in *what if* — the mental state where you wish a person, situation, your past, or anything else is different than it actually is. Signs that you're in a *What If* state include thinking

- I'll be happy when…
- I would be okay if…
- When I____ , then I can _____.
- If I only he or she would….

The problem with *what if* is that it imposes limitations on happiness, as if it's not possible to be happy unless certain conditions are met. The idea that you would be happy if you lost ten pounds, met the love of your life, got a different job, or had a certain amount of money is that those are external circumstances. If happiness is dependent upon things outside yourself, you end up powerless because you can't control the external, only your response to it.

If your boss, your client, your partner, your child, the cashier, or the car next to you in traffic has power over whether or not you're happy, your happiness blows like a balloon in the wind. It can be carried away, popped, or be outside your reach.

If your happiness exists independently of any outside condition being met, then no matter what happens, you can be happy. That doesn't mean a Pollyannaish approach to life where you gloss over bad things and are falsely optimistic. Instead, you can feel whatever feelings come up—

83

anger, sadness, desire, frustration, grief—and still be a happy person overall because happiness is more than an emotion. It is a state of being.

What are your *what ifs*, the things you keep thinking would give you happiness or might take your happiness away?

_____

_____

_____

_____

_____

_____

It is possible to accept yourself and your life as it is, to be happy with what is, and to continue to develop yourself. Instead of *what if*, you can empower yourself with conscious intentions and goals that you can work toward without giving your happiness over to them because "Happiness is an inside job," as William Arthur Ward claims.

Part of what you're doing in keeping a happiness journal is cultivating contentment: being with what is, feeling grateful and recognizing happiness in the moment. You've been building mindfulness skills throughout this book as you have bookmarked happiness, recognized when you're out of balance, and call yourself back to center. You can apply those skills to *what if* scenarios.

In any given situation, when you find yourself thinking *what if...*, bring yourself back to *what is*. What is happening right now? Do I need anything in this moment? How can I take care of myself? How does it feel to be in my body? What story am I telling myself right now? And then, stop. Look around. Breathe. Be right here.

You might even narrate to yourself what is happening. "I am worrying that... but right now I am looking out the window and there's a bird on the branch of my neighbor's tree." As you narrate, use your five senses to ground you in the world as it exists right now outside your head. This technique helps to manage anxiety, to halt storytelling, to bring yourself back to what is right here.

If you'd like a more structured approach, use the 54321 method: five things you see around you, four things you can touch, three things you can hear, two things you can smell, one thing you can taste. You can say them out loud, or if you're someplace where saying them out loud would add to your anxiety, do 54321 in your head.

Look back at your definition of happiness from week one of this journal. Is it a *what if* statement reliant on external conditions? If so, take a minute now to consider how you define happiness as an internal state, regardless of outside circumstances.

_____

_____

_____

_____

_____

_____

Date: __/__/__

Today, I'm looking forward to...

_____

_____

_____

Goals/Intentions for today:

_____

_____

_____

"Painful as it may be, a significant emotional event can be the catalyst for choosing a direction that serves us—and those around us—more effectively. Look for the learning."
– Louisa May Alcott

I felt happiest today when...

_____

_____

_____

Diversions from what I intended ...

_____

_____

_____

I'm grateful for...

_____

_____

_____

Plans for tomorrow:

_____   I am feeling:

_____

_____   ☺   ☺   ☹

86

Date: __/__/__

Today, I'm looking forward to...

_____
_____
_____

Goals/Intentions for today:

_____
_____
_____

"Happiness ...not in another place, but this place...
not for another hour, but this hour."
– Walt Whitman

I felt happiest today when...

_____
_____
_____

Diversions from what I intended ...

_____
_____
_____

I'm grateful for...

_____
_____
_____

Plans for tomorrow:

_____   I am feeling:
_____
_____   ☺   ☺   ☹

87

Date: __/__/__

Today, I'm looking forward to…

_____

_____

_____

Goals/Intentions for today:

_____

_____

_____

"You can't run away from yourself."
– Bob Marley

I felt happiest today when…

_____

_____

_____

Diversions from what I intended …

_____

_____

_____

I'm grateful for…

_____

_____

_____

Plans for tomorrow:

_____   I am feeling:

_____

_____   ☺ ☺ ☹

Today, I'm looking forward to…

_____

_____

_____

Goals/Intentions for today:

_____

_____

_____

"When someone shows you who they are,
believe them the first time."
– Maya Angelou

I felt happiest today when…

_____

_____

_____

Diversions from what I intended …

_____

_____

_____

I'm grateful for…

_____

_____

_____

Plans for tomorrow:

_____   I am feeling:

_____

_____   ☺   ☺   ☹

Date: __/__/__

Today, I'm looking forward to…

_____

_____

_____

Goals/Intentions for today:

_____

_____

_____

"Take the pearl. Leave the shell behind."
– Rumi

I felt happiest today when…

_____

_____

_____

Diversions from what I intended …

_____

_____

_____

I'm grateful for…

_____

_____

_____

Plans for tomorrow:

_____

_____   I am feeling:

_____
                                              ☺   ☺   ☹

Date: __/__/__

Today, I'm looking forward to…

_____

_____

_____

Goals/Intentions for today:

_____

_____

_____

"It is in you. Go and find it."
– Joseph Campbell

I felt happiest today when…

_____

_____

_____

Diversions from what I intended …

_____

_____

_____

I'm grateful for…

_____

_____

_____

Plans for tomorrow:

_____   I am feeling:

_____

_____   ☺   😐   ☹

Today, I'm looking forward to...

_____

_____

_____

Goals/Intentions for today:

_____

_____

_____

"Our very looking is the light feasting on the light."
– Li Young Lee

I felt happiest today when...

_____

_____

_____

Diversions from what I intended ...

_____

_____

_____

I'm grateful for...

_____

_____

_____

Plans for tomorrow:

_____

_____   I am feeling:

_____

☺   ☺   ☹

Cultivate New Habits: Good Days

Weekly Happiness Tool 10

When you're journaling daily, are there intentions or goals that you'd like to cultivate as daily or weekly habits: exercise, bedtime, seeing friends, restricting screen time, food/drink goals, doing activities from your play list, etc.?

_____   _____
_____   _____
_____   _____
_____   _____

What one thing could you change right now?

_____
_____
_____

What would it take to make it happen?

_____
_____
_____
_____
_____
_____

Date: __/__/__

Today, I'm looking forward to...

_____

_____

_____

Goals/Intentions for today:

_____

_____

_____

"Success is the sum of small efforts, repeated day in and day out."
– Robert Collier

I felt happiest today when...

_____

_____

_____

Diversions from what I intended ...

_____

_____

_____

I'm grateful for...

_____

_____

_____

Plans for tomorrow:

_____   I am feeling:

_____

_____   ☺   ☺   ☹

94

Date: __/__/__

Today, I'm looking forward to...

_____

_____

_____

Goals/Intentions for today:

_____

_____

_____

"Choose well: your choice is brief and yet endless."
– Ella Winter

I felt happiest today when...

_____

_____

_____

Diversions from what I intended ...

_____

_____

_____

I'm grateful for...

_____

_____

_____

Plans for tomorrow:

_____   I am feeling:

_____

_____   ☺   😐   ☹

Date: __/__/__

Today, I'm looking forward to…

_____

_____

_____

Goals/Intentions for today:

_____

_____

_____

"Act as if what you do makes a difference. It does."
– William James

I felt happiest today when…

_____

_____

_____

Diversions from what I intended …

_____

_____

_____

I'm grateful for…

_____

_____

_____

Plans for tomorrow:

_____   I am feeling:

_____

_____   ☺ ☺ ☹

Date: __/__/__

Today, I'm looking forward to...

_____

_____

_____

Goals/Intentions for today:

_____

_____

_____

"Things start as hopes and end up as habits."
– Lillian Hellman

I felt happiest today when...

_____

_____

_____

Diversions from what I intended ...

_____

_____

_____

I'm grateful for...

_____

_____

_____

Plans for tomorrow:

_____   I am feeling:

_____

_____   ☺   😐   ☹

97

Date: __/__/__

Today, I'm looking forward to...

_____

_____

_____

Goals/Intentions for today:

_____

_____

_____

"Success doesn't come from what you do occasionally,
it comes from what you do consistently."
– Marie Forleo

I felt happiest today when...

_____

_____

_____

Diversions from what I intended ...

_____

_____

_____

I'm grateful for...

_____

_____

_____

Plans for tomorrow:

_____   I am feeling:

_____

_____   ☺   😐   ☹

Date: __/__/__

Today, I'm looking forward to...

_____

_____

_____

Goals/Intentions for today:

_____

_____

_____

"No one saves us but ourselves. No one can and no one may.
We ourselves must walk the path."
– Buddha

I felt happiest today when...

_____

_____

_____

Diversions from what I intended ...

_____

_____

_____

I'm grateful for...

_____

_____

_____

Plans for tomorrow:

_____   I am feeling:

_____

_____   ☺   ☺   ☹

Today, I'm looking forward to…

_____

_____

_____

Goals/Intentions for today:

_____

_____

_____

"One may walk over the highest mountain one step at a time."
– John Wanamaker

I felt happiest today when…

_____

_____

_____

Diversions from what I intended …

_____

_____

_____

I'm grateful for…

_____

_____

_____

Plans for tomorrow:

_____   I am feeling:

_____

_____   ☺   😐   ☹

Pause Before Yes

Weekly Happiness Tool 11

When we say yes to something, we're saying yes to giving that thing time, energy, brain space, money, and/or priority. Sometimes saying yes is exactly the right choice, but before you do, think the *yes* through.

When someone (including you) asks you to do something, pause before you agree to it. Consider whether you like the *idea* of the thing or you'll like the reality of it. Do you even want to do it? If you do, still pause.

Think through what saying yes means. What does saying yes to a project at work or at home, a social commitment, volunteering your time, or donating your money entail? How much time will it take?

Consider not just how long doing the thing will take, but the time to get ready for it— if you must dress a certain way or prepare something. Will there be travel time to and from? Does the time of day impact the travel time?

What will saying yes to this thing mean for the rest of your day? Even if the whole day was free, if what you'd planned to do was have a quiet stay-at-home recharging day, that counts. Is there anything you won't be able to do or buy if you say yes to this thing?

Pausing before yes means you're making a well-thought out choice that considers all of the ramifications, even if it's just that watching another show will make you go to bed later than you intended so you might not do your before-bed routine, or you might feel sleepy and rushed the next morning.

101

Dr. Laura Markham says, "Self-discipline is giving up something you want to get something you want more." When you pause before you say yes, you're taking the time to ask yourself what you want and if there's anything you want more. Then, you're not so much depriving yourself by saying no to one thing as you are saying yes to what you want the most.

This helps you prioritize your goals are over your momentary urges. It also helps you consider the opportunity cost – the loss of potential gain in one area when you choose something else.

Pausing before you agree to something also helps you really mean yes when you do say it.

*In this pause between the happiness tool and your next gratitude page, a reminder that you've got two more weeks of this journal before you'll run out. You might want to say yes to ordering your next journal while you have plenty of time. See what I did there?

Date: __/__/__

Today, I'm looking forward to…

_____

_____

_____

Goals/Intentions for today:

_____

_____

_____

"This is your life. You are responsible for it.
You will not live forever. Don't wait."
– Natalie Goldberg

I felt happiest today when…

_____

_____

_____

Diversions from what I intended …

_____

_____

_____

I'm grateful for…

_____

_____

_____

Plans for tomorrow:

_____   I am feeling:

_____

_____   ☺   ☻   ☹

Date: __/__/__

Today, I'm looking forward to…

_____

_____

_____

Goals/Intentions for today:

_____

_____

_____

"You are what you do, not what you say you'll do."
– C.G. Jung

I felt happiest today when…

_____

_____

_____

Diversions from what I intended …

_____

_____

_____

I'm grateful for…

_____

_____

_____

Plans for tomorrow:

_____   I am feeling:

_____

_____   ☺   ☺   ☹

Today, I'm looking forward to...

_____

_____

_____

Goals/Intentions for today:

_____

_____

_____

"The more I want to get something done, the less I call it work."
– Richard Bach

I felt happiest today when...

_____

_____

_____

Diversions from what I intended ...

_____

_____

_____

I'm grateful for...

_____

_____

_____

Plans for tomorrow:

_____   I am feeling:

_____

_____   ☺   ☺   ☹

Date: __/__/__

Today, I'm looking forward to...

_____

_____

_____

Goals/Intentions for today:

_____

_____

_____

*"Responsibility to yourself means refusing to let others
do your thinking, talking, and naming for you."*
– Adrienne Rich

I felt happiest today when...

_____

_____

_____

Diversions from what I intended ...

_____

_____

_____

I'm grateful for...

_____

_____

_____

Plans for tomorrow:

_____   I am feeling:

_____

_____   ☺   ☺   ☹

Date: __/__/__

Today, I'm looking forward to...

_____

_____

_____

Goals/Intentions for today:

_____

_____

_____

"The price of anything is the amount of life you exchange for it."
– Henry David Thoreau

I felt happiest today when...

_____

_____

_____

Diversions from what I intended ...

_____

_____

_____

I'm grateful for...

_____

_____

_____

Plans for tomorrow:

_____   I am feeling:

_____

_____   ☺   ☺   ☹

Date: __/__/__

Today, I'm looking forward to...

_____

_____

_____

Goals/Intentions for today:

_____

_____

_____

*"The more room you give yourself to express your true thoughts and feelings,
the more room there is for your wisdom to emerge."*
– Marianne Williamson

I felt happiest today when...

_____

_____

_____

Diversions from what I intended ...

_____

_____

_____

I'm grateful for...

_____

_____

_____

Plans for tomorrow:

_____   I am feeling:

_____

_____   ☺   😐   ☹

Today, I'm looking forward to…

_____

_____

_____

Goals/Intentions for today:

_____

_____

_____

"Don't get so busy making a living if you forget to make a life."
– Dolly Parton

I felt happiest today when…

_____

_____

_____

Diversions from what I intended …

_____

_____

_____

I'm grateful for…

_____

_____

_____

Plans for tomorrow:

_____   I am feeling:

_____

_____   ☺   ☺   ☹

Define Enough

Weekly Happiness Tool 12

Enoughness is the state of being or having enough. Enough means "as much as you need." You've been practicing enoughness throughout this book as you've noticed what you're grateful for, whether it's the sunshine coming in the window, hitting all the green lights, or connecting with a friend. We might call that *enoughness* satisfaction, contentment, or acceptance.

When people look at themselves, the *enough* standard often gets twisted into good enough, successful enough, skinny enough. Or they look at their homes, jobs, possessions, or calendars and think they're not successful, wealthy, or busy enough.

What is *enough*? You don't need to look at every area of your life and define specifics. Instead, stop to question what enough feels like. What does enough represent? What would enough mean for your life?

_____

_____

_____

_____

_____

_____

_____

_____

Take a minute to write down the not-good-enough messages that swim around in your head. What part of yourself or your life are you telling yourself isn't enough?

_____

_____

_____

_____

_____

_____

_____

_____

What would it take to look at your life through the lens of enough, to see yourself and what you have and do as enough, without any need to change?

_____

_____

_____

_____

_____

_____

_____

_____

*A reminder that you're almost done with this journal. Be sure to order your next one while you have _enough_ time. Yep, I did it again.

Today, I'm looking forward to…

_____

_____

_____

Goals/Intentions for today:

_____

_____

_____

"Happiness is a place between too little and too much."
– Finnish Proverb

I felt happiest today when…

_____

_____

_____

Diversions from what I intended …

_____

_____

_____

I'm grateful for…

_____

_____

_____

Plans for tomorrow:

_____   I am feeling:

_____

_____   ☺   ☺   ☹

Today, I'm looking forward to…

_____

_____

_____

Goals/Intentions for today:

_____

_____

_____

"The best is the enemy of the good."
– Voltaire

I felt happiest today when…

_____

_____

_____

Diversions from what I intended …

_____

_____

_____

I'm grateful for…

_____

_____

_____

Plans for tomorrow:

_____   I am feeling:

_____

_____   ☺   ☺   ☹

Today, I'm looking forward to...

_____

_____

_____

Goals/Intentions for today:

_____

_____

_____

"Just work to love yourself as much as you can —
not more than the people around you but not so much less."
– Sharon Olds

I felt happiest today when...

_____

_____

_____

Diversions from what I intended ...

_____

_____

_____

I'm grateful for...

_____

_____

_____

Plans for tomorrow:

_____   I am feeling:

_____

_____   ☺ ☺ ☹

Today, I'm looking forward to…

_____

_____

_____

Goals/Intentions for today:

_____

_____

_____

"Trying to be happy by accumulating possessions is like trying
to satisfy hunger by taping sandwiches all over your body."
– George Carlin

I felt happiest today when…

_____

_____

_____

Diversions from what I intended …

_____

_____

_____

I'm grateful for…

_____

_____

_____

Plans for tomorrow:

_____   I am feeling:

_____

_____   ☺   ☺   ☹

Today, I'm looking forward to…

_____

_____

_____

Goals/Intentions for today:

_____

_____

_____

"Perfection is highly overrated.
Real learning and growth come with imperfection."
– Felicia Watlington

I felt happiest today when…

_____

_____

_____

Diversions from what I intended …

_____

_____

_____

I'm grateful for…

_____

_____

_____

Plans for tomorrow:

_____   I am feeling:

_____

_____   ☺   ☺   ☹

Today, I'm looking forward to...

_____

_____

_____

Goals/Intentions for today:

_____

_____

_____

"And did you get what you wanted from this life, even so?"
– Raymond Carver

I felt happiest today when...

_____

_____

_____

Diversions from what I intended ...

_____

_____

_____

I'm grateful for...

_____

_____

_____

Plans for tomorrow:

_____   I am feeling:

_____

_____   ☺ ☺ ☹

Today, I'm looking forward to...

_____

_____

_____

Goals/Intentions for today:

_____

_____

_____

"Finish each day and be done with it. You have done what you could.
Some blunders and absurdities no doubt crept in; forget them as soon as you can.
Tomorrow is a new day. You shall begin it serenely and with too high a spirit
to be encumbered with your old nonsense."
– R.W. Emerson

I felt happiest today when...

_____

_____

_____

Diversions from what I intended ...

_____

_____

_____

I'm grateful for...

_____

_____

_____

Plans for tomorrow:

_____   I am feeling:

_____

_____   ☺ ☺ ☹

118

Reflecting

Weekly Happiness Tool 13

You've been engaged in a gratitude practice for three months. Six minutes a day can add up to a lot of change.

How is noticing what you're happy and grateful for each day impacting your life?

_____

_____

_____

What have you noticed about diversions from your intentions?

_____

_____

_____

What are your goals for your next three months?

_____

_____

_____

As a thank you and to help you expand your gratitude practice, go to spacewiseorganizing.com/thankyougift to download 25 gratitude practices that you can use along with the journal or in your everyday life with family, friends, and random strangers out in the world. Enjoy!

Acknowledgments

This book was inspired by the happiness support and accountability groups I lead for women. I created this first for you. Thanks also to Kate Martin for technical advice, and to Stephanie Gipson, Lisa Appleby, Cassandra Jones, and Darren German for editing, feedback, and for being my first readers. Any mistakes remaining are my own.

Made in the USA
Coppell, TX
21 December 2019

13618792R00075